war

THE WORLD REACTS

Paul Bennett

Belitha Press

FOREWORD

Disasters affect all of us. At some point in life, everyone has a good chance of either being caught in one or knowing someone who is.

For many people, the disaster may be a car crash or a house fire, and the police, firefighters or ambulance service will be on hand to help. But for millions of people around the world, disasters happen far more often and are more catastrophic.

Some countries suffer frequent natural disasters such as floods, earthquakes and droughts. They do not always have the resources to deal with the crisis, and it is usually the poorest people who are the most affected and least able to recover.

War is a man-made disaster that ruins people's lives. The effects of droughts and floods are made worse when there is war.

When people are unable to cope with a disaster, they need the help of relief agencies such as the Red Cross. Relief agencies react quickly to emergencies, bringing help to those in need. Many times, people are not even aware of disasters in other countries until international aid is discussed on the news.

War: The World Reacts ties in closely with the work of the International Federation of Red Cross and Red Crescent Societies. The Federation coordinates international disaster relief and promotes development around the world to prevent and alleviate human suffering. There is a Red Cross or Red Crescent society in almost every country of the world. Every year we help millions of people affected by disasters.

This book will help readers understand the problems faced by people threatened by disaster. It will also explain what can be done to help.

George Weber
Former Secretary General
International Federation of Red Cross
and Red Crescent Societies

◀ *The Red Cross symbol (left) was first created to protect the wounded in war and those who cared for them. The Red Crescent symbol (right) is used by Muslim countries around the world. Both symbols have equal status.*

CONTENTS

Words in **bold** appear in the
glossary on page 31.

WHAT IS WAR?

War is a violent argument between countries. It can also be between different sides within a country – this is called civil war.

Why do wars happen?

We often see pictures on the news of soldiers fighting. But why do soldiers try to kill or injure each other?

Wars happen for many reasons. They may start because a country wants more land and power, and so it **invades** another country. They may be fought over resources such as good farmland or land that is rich in oil or gold.

Wars also start because of differences in religion or because one group in a country wants to gain power over another group.

▼ *A Cambodian girl carries a rifle. Girls are sometimes forced to fight in armed conflicts.*

Wars in the 20th century

There have been wars throughout history. There were two world wars in the 20th century – the First World War (1914–18) and the Second World War (1939–45) – that involved many different countries.

After the Second World War there was a period of hostility between the United States and its western **allies** and the former **Soviet Union** and its eastern allies. Called the Cold War, this was a time when the two power blocs threatened to attack each other, each with powerful armed forces.

The two power blocs dominated world affairs in both military and diplomatic terms. As a result, little attention was paid to wars in the poor countries of the world.

Wars today

By the end of the 1980s, the Cold War was over. This was followed by the Gulf War (1990–91), led by the United States, as a result of Iraq's invasion of Kuwait. Despite this war, many people hoped there would be a new age of peace. More attention was being paid to the causes of civil war in the world's poorest countries in Central and South America, Africa, and Asia and the Far East. Although most of today's wars are civil wars fought between groups within a country, wars also start as a result of **terrorist** attacks like the one on the United States on 11 September 2001.

▲ *The World Trade Center is engulfed in flames after two airliners crash into it in a terrorist attack on 11 September 2001.*

Aid in action

War: The World Reacts describes what happens when there is a war, and shows how the world can help. It looks at wars around the world and at the assistance given by governments and **relief agencies**.

This book tries to help you understand why wars happen and how ordinary people are affected. It will show you how the victims of war are helped and how important peace is for everyone.

PEOPLE ON THE MOVE

When war breaks out, people leave their homes to escape the fighting. This means thousands of people may be on the move.

Travelling in safety

People leave their villages for the safety of towns and cities, or they cross the border into another country.

They may be driven from their homes by **ethnic** cleansing, which is when one group of people tries to force all other ethnic groups out of an area. Ethnic cleansing, which is a goal in many civil wars, has led to the killing of whole communities.

Governments and relief agencies try to make sure that people escaping conflict can travel in safety. This may be difficult since some countries do not want outside forces interfering with their problems and will not let them in. Relief agencies may find it impossible to help people. Often, people only find protection once they cross a border and enter another country.

▼ *Refugees from Zaire travel by boat across Lake Tanganyika to find safety in neighbouring Tanzania.*

Who is a refugee?
Refugees are people who have been forced to leave their country – often because they fear for their lives. They give up their homes, jobs and families to find safety.

The office of the **United Nations** High Commissioner for Refugees (UNHCR) began its work in 1951. It was set up to help people who had fled their country. Now it also helps internally displaced people – people who have fled because of war or fear of persecution but have not crossed the border into another country.

Yugoslavia 1991–92

Fleeing the fighting

In 1991–92, Yugoslavia split apart when some of the **republics** that made up Yugoslavia, including Croatia, Slovenia, Bosnia and Macedonia, announced that they were now **independent** countries. Fights over land broke out almost immediately between groups.

Millions on the move

During the next five years, four million people were forced to leave their homes – the biggest movement of people in Europe since the Second World War. Thousands were killed through ethnic cleansing. One group of people, the Serbs, were responsible for most of the ethnic cleansing.

▲ *War disrupts everyday life. In many cities in the former Yugoslavia, children couldn't travel to school because of the danger of being shot.*

Amra, a 13-year-old Bosnian refugee, remembers how she became separated from her sister, Elma, during the war:

"The war broke out and I saw many people killed. . . . My mother told us we should go to Croatia. She tried to fetch Elma, but there was an explosion and she couldn't reach her. . . . We lived in a refugee center in Croatia for two months. One day some people came and asked us if we wanted to go to Switzerland. So we left Croatia."

This Bosnian child was forced to leave his home because of fighting.

7

SAFETY FOR CIVILIANS

When there is war, innocent people need protection. The **United Nations** (UN) tries to protect **civilians** by setting up safe areas in war zones.

Safe havens

Safe havens are places in a war zone that are free from fighting. People go to these areas to find safety and to get help from relief agencies, which provide them with food, water, medicine and shelter.

Safe areas are a good idea, but they do not always work. They are rarely set up with the agreement of all sides in a war, and soldiers are sometimes allowed into these areas. This means that they are often a target for attack by warring groups, making them far from safe. With this threat of attack, relief agencies may find it difficult to help civilians in a safe zone.

Staying neutral
It is important that relief agencies remain neutral – that they do not favour one warring group over another. The International Committee of the Red Cross (ICRC) has a special role to help the victims of war – civilians, wounded soldiers and **prisoners of war** – on both sides of a conflict. Other relief agencies are also neutral. They know that the success of their work depends on not taking sides. But not everyone accepts the neutrality of relief agencies, and often they are not allowed into a country to help victims of war.

▼ *UN troops guard a safe haven for Kurdish refugees near the Turkish–Iraqi border. The Kurds fled because they feared Iraqi attacks.*

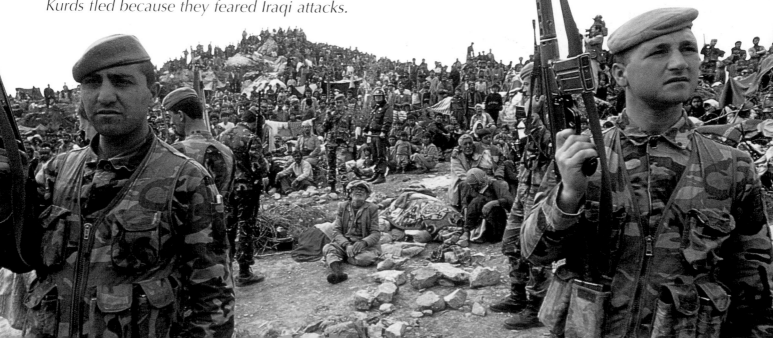

Rwanda 1994

Helping both sides

When civil war broke out in Rwanda in 1994, it was difficult for relief agencies to protect civilians and to appear neutral.

Conflict between the Hutu and Tutsi groups in the country began in April 1994 when the Hutu president of Rwanda was killed, and Hutus blamed Tutsis for the killing. More than half a million Tutsis were then killed by the Hutus.

The Tutsis retaliated, and the Hutus were forced to leave Rwanda. In a matter of days, more than two million Hutus crossed the borders into Zaire, Tanzania and Burundi.

▲ *A Rwandan family loads belongings into a truck and flees the country.*

▲ *A Rwandan boy, separated from his family during civil war, is protected by a United Nations soldier.*

Caught in the crossfire

Relief agencies were caught between the rival groups, but they had to help the Hutu refugees, some of whom had killed Tutsis.

The United Nations set up safe areas in Rwanda. More than one million people, mainly Hutus, found protection in a safe zone in southwestern Rwanda.

As the months passed, the Tutsi-led government became impatient for people to return home. It saw the camps, mainly inhabited by Hutus, as a threat. So, in April 1995, the government started moving people home. People in the camps were threatened with guns, and about 3000 were killed. Some people say that this was **revenge** for the **massacre** of Tutsis that had taken place a year earlier.

AID IN A WAR ZONE

Bringing emergency aid to people in a war zone is a huge job that can be dangerous.

Organizing relief

Relief agencies need permission from warring sides to give **aid** in a war zone. Even when this permission is given, relief workers are often stopped and threatened by soldiers. There is also the danger that relief agency vehicles, radios, food and medical supplies will be stolen by an army for its own use.

The delivery of aid needs a lot of organization and cooperation between the groups involved. Relief agencies must work together to prevent delays that would increase the suffering. Sometimes relief agencies divide tasks between them. For example, one agency looks after the water supplies, another looks after toilets and medical care and another is responsible for providing food.

▲ *A young Iraqi boy balances a pot of fresh water bags sent by the Red Cross during the* **Gulf War**.

Aid under fire

Bringing aid to a war zone can be very dangerous. Relief workers are often caught in the middle of the fighting, so they sometimes wear bullet-proof vests to protect themselves (left). Violence may be used against them if they are seen as taking sides in a conflict, or they may be taken **hostage** by one of the warring groups. Some Red Cross workers have been murdered while trying to help war victims, causing relief agencies to think very hard about their role in times of conflict.

Somalia 1994

Fighting clans

The civil war in Somalia began in 1988. A large part of the population was forced to cross the border into neighbouring countries, where relief camps were set up. Farmers could no longer tend their crops because of the conflict, and **drought** and war at the same time caused food shortages and famine.

Controlling aid

Relief agencies had difficulties delivering aid to Somalians because of the number of tribal groups, or clans, fighting each other. Everything had to be done through local **warlords**, who controlled the law and order. Even in relief camps, food supplies were controlled by clan leaders. Relief workers were accused of favouring one clan over another, and fighting often broke out in the camps.

▲ *This Somalian soldier waits for a delivery of food aid by truck. Warlords made the delivery of aid almost impossible.*

Overcoming the obstacles

Despite all these difficulties, relief agencies have continued to help the people of Somalia. **Médecins Sans Frontières (MSF)**, for example, opened a clinic in the Bakool area of the country. Twelve Somali relief workers and an MSF nurse now work at the centre.

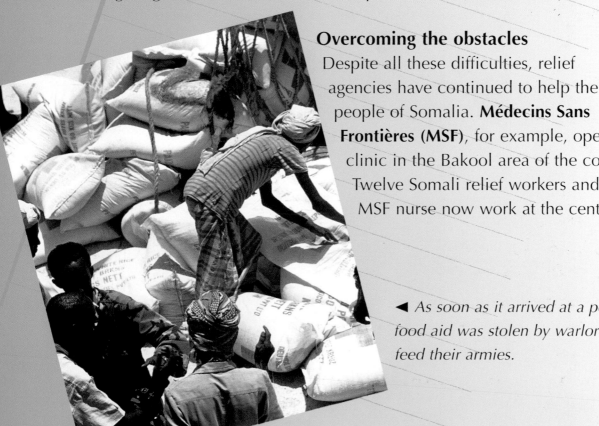

◀ *As soon as it arrived at a port, food aid was stolen by warlords to feed their armies.*

APPEALS FOR AID

Aid supplies run short as more and more people arrive at relief camps. Soon, more help is needed.

Emergency response

Relief agencies send in emergency response teams to assess the needs of people in relief camps. Some people may have walked for days to reach a camp and are weak when they arrive. Others may have bullet or bomb wounds that need urgent treatment.

People need emergency food and water. They also need tents for shelter, as well as blankets and clothes to keep them warm.

Relief agencies work hard to give out food supplies and to care for the sick and wounded. They dig toilets and drill wells for water. People need clean and safe water as quickly as possible, because dirty water often carries diseases.

Some relief agencies keep aid supplies ready to ship to other countries when an emergency arises. Sometimes the United Nations and its agencies make appeals to governments around the world for their help.

War and famine

War is one of the main causes of famine. It forces farmers to abandon their crops and animals. Whole harvests are left to rot as people leave their homes to escape the fighting.

When the rains do not come, harvests fail and people go hungry. When there is drought and war at the same time, the result is nearly always famine.

During a food shortage, prices rise and people have to pay more for less food. People fleeing conflict often can't afford to buy any food. Without help from relief agencies, they may starve.

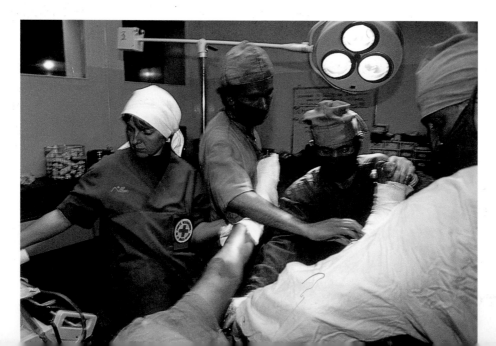

◀ *Red Cross doctors and nurses are sent into war zones to save lives. Here they are treating an injured person in a hospital in Kabul, the war-torn capital of Afghanistan.*

Chechnya 1994

Appeal for aid

After the end of the Cold War, many republics of the former Soviet Union wanted to rule themselves. Chechnya was one of the republics that wanted independence; this led to fighting with the government of Russia.

▲ *Russian troops patrol the ruins of Grozny, Chechnya's capital city.*

Crossing borders

In December 1994, Russian government forces crossed the border into Chechnya. Many people died in the fighting that followed, and hundreds of thousands fled into neighbouring republics.

An appeal for help

The Russian government asked for help to cope with the mass movement of people that occurred after Russian troops went in. In January 1995, the United Nations High Commissioner for Refugees sent workers to Chechnya to assess the emergency. A month later, there was an appeal to countries around the world for donations.

Help at hand

The money raised was spent on shelters, toilets and stoves and pots for cooking. Some of the money was also spent on improving health care.

The war in Chechnya ended in 1996. Since then the people have enjoyed only limited freedom to rule themselves. A new war broke out in 1999.

▶ *Children in Grozny play in front of their bombed school.*

RELIEF CONVOYS

Convoys of trucks may have to travel long distances to deliver aid to a war zone. Their journey is sometimes made difficult by road blocks and the threat of attack.

Moving supplies

Delivering relief supplies to a war zone is a difficult job. Ports, roads and railroads may be damaged, and supplies have to be flown to more remote areas.

Most aid is sent by ship and delivered to ports. But if a country is not on the coast, supplies have to travel through neighbouring countries. Railroads are the best way of moving supplies overland, because thousands of tonnes can be moved on a single journey. But trains only run on certain routes and cannot deliver to every village.

Convoys of trucks, which can travel almost anywhere by road, are often used to transport aid.

▼ *The United Nations protects a convoy of trucks delivering aid to a war zone.*

Red Cross food parcels
The Red Cross is famous for the food parcels it distributes. What goes into a parcel depends on the country it is going to; the contents have to suit the people's diet. For example, in Georgia, one of the former Soviet republics, the parcels were made up of 6 kg (13 pounds) of flour, 3 kg (7 pounds) of rice, 2 kg (4 pounds) of sugar, 2 kg (4 pounds) of kidney beans, 2 kg (4 pounds) of pasta, 2 litres (0.5 gallons) of vegetable oil, 100 g (3 ounces) of yeast, 600 g (20 ounces) of canned beef, 600 g (20 ounces) of soap, and candles and matches. Each parcel fed one person for two months.

Sudan 1991

Shipping the aid

There has been civil war in Sudan since 1983. Many people have been displaced and killed, and food supplies have also been stolen. Years of drought in the early 1990s combined with war to bring famine to Sudan.

▲ Food aid is unloaded at Port Sudan. The 4000-km (2400-mile) journey from northern Europe took one month.

A ship's journey

The Dutch Red Cross sent food supplies to the victims of war and famine in 1991. Its ship, the *Darfur*, left Rotterdam in Holland on May 2 and headed down the coast of France, around Spain and into the Mediterranean Sea. It then sailed through the Suez Canal and the Red Sea, arriving

in Port Sudan on June 2.

Moving the aid

The *Darfur* docked and was unloaded as quickly as possible. Supplies were then moved by rail or road. About 8800 tonnes of aid went by rail to Khartoum – the capital of Sudan – each month, and truck convoys took more there by road.

From Khartoum, food supplies were driven to distribution centres in the southern part of the country. People came to these centres to collect the food.

▼ From the ship, sacks of grain are loaded on to trucks.

KEEPING THE PEACE

Only peace can bring people hope for the future. The United Nations plays an important role in bringing peace to war-torn countries.

The United Nations

Since the end of the Cold War, the world has turned more and more to the United Nations to deal with conflicts. The UN encourages warring sides to stop fighting and to build a peaceful future together.

The Security Council is the part of the UN responsible for peacekeeping. With the agreement of warring sides, it oversees peace agreements and **cease-fires** and tries to stop disagreements between groups from turning into full-scale war. The Council also has the power to bring **sanctions**, or penalties, against warring countries.

UN soldiers, known by their blue helmets, are often used for peacekeeping. They carry weapons, but they can only use them in special circumstances to defend themselves. The UN also works to make sure that **elections** are carried out fairly and without violence.

▼ *The UN monitored 1993 Cambodian elections to make sure that they were carried out fairly.*

Human rights

Treaties are agreements by different countries to obey the same law. Some treaties protect **human rights**. These include laws against **racism**, cruel treatment or punishment of people, and laws to protect children.

In a war zone, these laws are often ignored. Part of the work of the United Nations is to penalize people who break these laws and to restore human rights.

For example, in the former Yugoslavia, the United Nations continues to watch over certain areas to make sure that human rights are protected.

Iraq 1991
Protecting the Kurds

Although Kurdish people have lived in Iraq for thousands of years, they have not been allowed to keep their own language and culture there.

After the Gulf War of 1990–91, there was a Kurdish **uprising** against the Iraqi government. It was unsuccessful, and about one and a half million Kurds, fearing Iraqi attacks, fled for the Turkish–Iraqi border.

Kurdish human rights

Because Iraq had ignored Kurdish human rights in the past, the United Nations decided to set up a safe area without agreement from the Iraqi government. Iraq had used **chemical weapons** against the Kurds in 1988, killing many women and children. The UN also brought economic sanctions – restrictions on trade with other countries – against Iraq at the beginning of the Gulf War when Iraq invaded Kuwait.

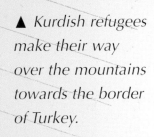

▲ *Kurdish refugees make their way over the mountains towards the border of Turkey.*

Iraq, which opposed the UN's actions, **blockaded** the safe haven and prevented relief agencies from entering. Relief agencies tried to distance themselves from the UN, hoping that Iraq would let them do their work. This didn't happen, and agencies had to bring in supplies without Iraqi permission.

◄ *Relief agencies deliver water to Kurdish refugees in the UN safe zone.*

REUNITING FAMILIES

Many of the refugees in a war zone are children on their own. They get split up from their families and may end up far away from home.

Tracing programs

Once the fighting is over, children need to be reunited with their families as soon as possible. Relief agencies such as the Red Cross run tracing programmes to help children find their relatives.

Agencies begin their work by registering the children and finding out what happened to them. Once they know a child's name and the area she came from, they can start trying to trace her parents or relatives – by using photos and radio messages and by visiting her home area.

This is not easy. Family members may have fled their homes or been killed in the fighting. Sometimes parents or relatives cannot be traced, and substitute parents are found to look after a child until she is grown and can take care of herself.

Basic rights

An international agreement, called the Convention on the Rights of the Child, gives everyone under the age of 18 the right to safety, shelter, food, water, health and education. Many countries have signed this treaty, but children still lack these rights. Many children – like the Bosnian child who drew the picture above – experience war first-hand.

When they become refugees in another country, children lose the protection of their government. Many lose the protection of their families too. This is why the Convention tries to protect the rights of refugee children around the world.

◄ *This Rwandan girl holds up her registration number. This photo will be used to try to trace her family.*

Afghanistan 1995

Searching for an uncle

Afghanistan has been in the grip of civil war since 1988. During an attack on the capital city of Kabul in 1995, a 10-year-old boy named Ghulam Nabi escaped unhurt when his house was flattened by an artillery shell. But his father and brother were both killed in the attack.

In the confusion that followed, Ghulam fled to Kandahar, where he ended up in a school. He couldn't remember anything about his journey or how he got there.

He wanted to return to Kabul and join his only living relative, his uncle, so he went to the **Red Crescent** for help.

Ten-year-old Ghulam was reunited with his uncle by the Red Crescent.

The tracing trail

The Afghan Red Crescent took Ghulam's name, age and his uncle's name and address. They also gathered details about where his uncle worked in case his uncle's home had been destroyed.

This information was sent to the Red Crescent in Kabul, where a case worker traced Ghulam's uncle. The uncle was told what had happened to his nephew and that Ghulam wanted to come and live with him. The Red Crescent then flew Ghulam to Kabul, where he was reunited with his uncle.

◀ Tanks in the war-torn capital of Kabul.

RETURNING HOME

When the war is over, refugees are encouraged to return home as soon as possible. But before they return home, they must know they can travel safely.

After the fighting

The journey home may be a long one by foot, so returnees – people returning home – are given supplies for their journey. Relief agencies set up way stations where people receive food, water and medical help on the way home.

Sometimes refugees are allowed to stay in the country they have fled to. Relief agencies may help them build new lives there, but only with the government's permission. Often permission is denied because the country is poor and cannot support thousands of refugees.

Refugees may also go to another country that is willing to take them for a short time on the condition that they resettle somewhere else in the future.

► *A Rwandan woman and her son return home after five months in a refugee camp in Zaire.*

Migrants or refugees?

Migrants are people who leave their country to seek a better life and more money in another country. Unlike refugees, they do not fear for their lives and may return home whenever they wish. According to the **Universal Declaration of Human Rights**, everyone has the right to seek refuge (a place of safety) and should not be returned to a country where their lives are in danger. Still, people are often refused refuge because governments suspect they are migrants.

Myanmar 1997

Going home

In recent years, 250 000 refugees have left Bangladesh to return home to Myanmar (formerly known as Burma) in the largest **repatriation** ever organized in Asia.

The Rohingya people are a **minority group** in Myanmar. They first entered Bangladesh in 1991–92 to escape **persecution** in their country. Some crossed the mountains into Bangladesh by foot or on bicycles; others travelled there by boat.

Bangladesh is one of the world's poorest countries and had very few resources to provide for the refugees. But with the help of relief agencies, about 20 camps were set up throughout the country to provide homes for tens of thousands of Rohingyas.

▲ *A UNHCR worker (centre) accompanies a widow and her children returning to Myanmar.*

Leaving Bangladesh

The Myanmar government agreed to take the Rohingyas back in 1997. The United Nations High Commissioner for Refugees (UNHCR) went with them to make sure that they had a safe journey back.

The UNHCR also helped people once they had arrived home. Many of the returnees had never learned to write their own language before they fled to Bangladesh, so UNHCR helped to fund projects to teach them. It also set up projects to repair schools and hospitals and gave small loans to people to restart their own businesses in some of the traditional crafts of pot-making and basket-weaving.

▲ *Returnee women weaving baskets from cane bamboo.*

REBUILDING LIVES

Returnees are given advice and help to rebuild their lives. Those who are resettled need support to help them adapt to a new life in a new country.

A new start

Returnees are given help to start again. They are given basic items such as cooking pots, salt and soap. Farmers are given tools and seed so that they can start to grow their own food again. People who live near lakes or rivers are given fishing nets so they can provide extra food for their families.

Training is also given so people can help themselves. This includes training in raising farm animals, **irrigation** and ways to control crop-eating **pests**.

Refugees who have been resettled in another country may find it difficult to make a new start. Often they do not know the language

▲ *Education is important to help children lead a normal life again.*

and customs of the country. Without help in learning the language and adapting to the way of life, it may be difficult for them to settle in their new home.

Child soldiers

The Convention on the Rights of the Child says that children under 15 years of age should never take part in war. But across the world, there are soldiers as young as six fighting on the front line. Child soldiers (left) may have been kidnapped and forced to fight, or they may have lost their parents in war and joined the army's 'family' to get food, clothing and shelter. Whatever the reasons, the effects on children of fighting in a war are very damaging. Those who survive often suffer from nightmares or become aggressive or withdrawn.

Cambodia 1993

Starting again

For many years, the people of Cambodia have had very little peace. Civil war, changes in government, and invasion by other countries have caused the deaths of millions of people, and many hundreds of thousands have fled the country.

More than 240 000 people went to live in refugee camps in Thailand. Between 1992 and 1993, all of these refugees returned to Cambodia with the help of the United Nations. Some were given tools and a plot of farmland; others were given food and loans to start again.

But many of the refugees who had hoped to return as farmers have been unable to farm the land – too much of the Cambodian countryside is littered with **land mines**.

▲ *These Cambodian children, born in Thailand, see their country for the first time from a train window.*

Many Cambodian children were born in Thai camps and have never seen their own country. Others, like 13-year-old Narin, spent most of their lives in refugee camps in Thailand:

"For most of my life, my home was Site 2, a big refugee camp in Thailand. But Site 2 was not that bad. I studied very hard, because education leads to a good job. My mother and father left us, and so now I live in an orphanage. I wish I could have my family back."

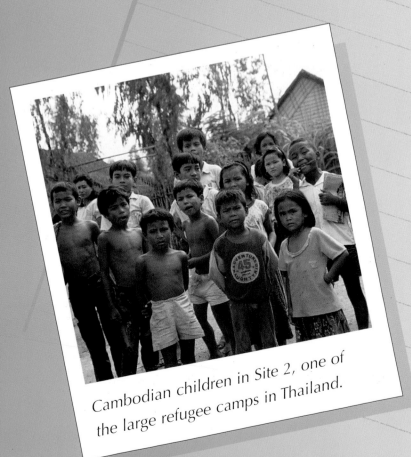

Cambodian children in Site 2, one of the large refugee camps in Thailand.

DANGEROUS MINES

Land mines are explosives that are placed in the ground in war zones. Many innocent people are killed or injured when they step on these mines.

People at risk

Land mines are laid in the ground by hand or scattered from the air during wartime. They are supposed to be a weapon against soldiers, but they threaten innocent people long after the fighting has ended.

Children, who run around and play on land that has been mined, are particularly at risk. Because they are small, their bodies are close to the blast. This means that their injuries are often worse than those of adults.

There are about 119 million unexploded mines in 71 countries worldwide. The most affected countries are Cambodia, Angola, Afghanistan and the former Yugoslavia.

Clearing mines is a huge job. Trained people risk their lives to dig them out and deactivate them. Many governments support mine clearance, but two million new mines are laid each year in war zones around the world, so clearing them is a huge task.

◄ *Digging out a land mine is slow and dangerous work.*

Banning land mines

The only solution to the problem of land mines is to ban them so that no one makes or uses them. Such a ban has at last become a possibility. An international treaty to ban land mines was signed in December 1997 by more than 120 countries. The countries that signed the treaty now hope that every country in the world will eventually sign.

Angola 1997

Living with land mines

After 20 years of civil war in Angola, peace has now given people a chance to rebuild their lives. But there are nine million land mines scattered across the country – one mine for each person. This is a major problem that people will face for years to come.

More than 70 000 Angolans have lost limbs through land mine explosions, and at least the same number have died. Two-thirds of the victims are young people between 16 and 30 years old.

Land mines have a devastating effect on people's lives. Injured people are unable to work and find it difficult to support themselves and their families. Mines also prevent good land from being farmed.

▶ *An Angolan girl learns to walk again using a false leg.*

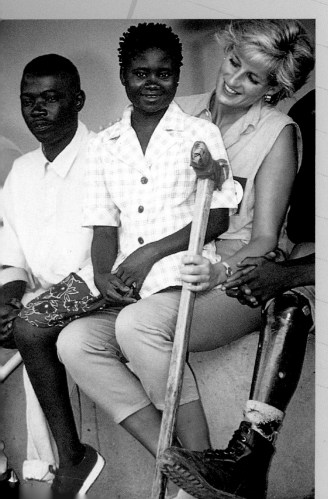

Helping land mine victims

Relief agencies provide medical help and equipment for land mine victims in Angola and other countries around the world. They run workshops that make false limbs and centres where victims are fitted with the limbs and taught to walk again.

The late Princess Diana of Wales visited Red Cross workshops in Angola in January 1997, eight months before her death. Her visit helped to attract worldwide attention to the suffering caused by land mines.

◀ *Princess Diana visits land mine victims in Angola in 1997.*

WORKING FOR PEACE

Poor people are made poorer by the effects of war. Relief agencies give emergency help in war zones and work to prevent conflicts in the future.

Preventing conflict

In many countries, there has been little improvement in the lives of the poorest people. People continue to suffer bad health from a lack of food and clean drinking water and still live in poor housing. As we have seen, the unhappiness that poverty brings creates a greater risk of conflict in these countries.

Relief agencies help to improve people's lives by supporting long-term projects. These projects help local people to grow food, improve water supplies and earn a living. This long-term aid gives people more independence and helps them to build for the future.

Relief agencies are also working to bring an end to the arms trade. Millions of cheap weapons are sold to the poorer nations of the world. Relief agencies also want countries to adopt trade policies that encourage peace in these countries. These are all ways of preventing conflict in the future.

The Red Cross

The Red Cross is the world's largest organization that cares for people in peace and war. There are national Red Cross and Red Crescent Societies in almost every country of the world, caring for people locally and abroad. The International Committee of the Red Cross (ICRC) helps the victims of war during and after the fighting. The International Federation of Red Cross and Red Crescent Societies gives aid in areas affected by natural disasters.

◀ *A United Nations soldier at a checkpoint in war-torn Somalia.*

Tajikistan 1993
Heading for home

Civil war broke out in Tajikistan in late 1992, soon after it became independent from the former Soviet Union. The fighting was mainly in the southwest part of the country, and by January 1993, the conflict had ended.

Although the civil war did not last long, the fighting was very brutal and forced more than one million people – one-fifth of the population – to leave their homes. More than 65 000 Tajiks crossed the border into neighbouring Afghanistan because they feared being killed.

▲ *A widow and her children stand in front of the ruins that were once their home.*

An end to the conflict

When the war ended, people began to return to their villages, but many found that their belongings had been stolen or their homes had been burned down.

The United Nations High Commissioner for Refugees helped refugees in Afghanistan to cross the border back into Tajikistan and provided building materials to rebuild homes destroyed by the civil war. By 1997, most of the people had returned home.

▲ *After the fighting, farmers returned to their fields to start growing crops again.*

NEW CHALLENGES

The wars that have broken out since the end of the Cold War have led to new challenges for relief agencies, resulting in new policies and different ways of helping.

Complicated crises

Today's emergencies are usually complicated. They often include civil war, the mass movement of people, changes in governments, disputes over borders, and, in many cases, drought and famine.

Relief organizations have had to find better ways of dealing with these crises. All those involved in disaster relief – governments, relief agencies and international organizations – now work together to help in an emergency. A **Code of Conduct** has been created for everyone to follow when responding to a disaster. But for the Code to work, the country receiving help must respect the work of the agencies. If the agencies are seen as taking sides, it will prevent them from helping people caught up in disaster.

▲ *During war, soldiers take food that is meant for civilians.*

Relief and development

Poverty is one of the main causes of civil war in many countries of the world. Poor living conditions, lack of food and water and the feeling of being powerless all create tension and unrest.

For these reasons, development – long-term ways of increasing people's standard of living – is important both for the prevention of conflict and for long-term peace.

Afghanistan 2001
War on terrorism

On 11 September 2001, **terrorists** hijacked passenger airplanes and flew them into the Twin Towers in New York and the Pentagon in Washington. Thousands of people from many different countries died in the attack.

The United States, supported by its **allies**, declared war on the terrorists and the countries that supported the terrorists. Afghanistan was identified as protecting Osama bin Laden, the leader of the terrorists responsible for the 11 September attack.

▲ *A boy walks near a Northern Alliance tank. Ordinary people suffered in the fighting to oust the Taliban and bring the terrorists to justice.*

The ruling Talibans (which had dominated the country since 1996) refused to give up the terrorist leader. The United States responded by bombing the Taliban army and by supporting the Northern Alliance forces opposed to Taliban rule. The fighting that ensued led to a flood of refugees to Pakistan and other countries bordering Afghanistan. With winter on the way, the fear of millions of people dying from cold and starvation prompted the aid agencies to send tents, food and other aid.

▲ *A delivery of food aid to a ruined town in Afghanistan.*

HOW YOU CAN HELP

War destroys people's lives.
Only peace can bring people
hope for the future.

● Make a poster for your school showing aspects of the world's refugee problem. Find out where the main refugee populations are and mark them on a world map.

● Choose a relief agency you would like to raise money for. Organize a fund-raising activity such as a sponsored bike ride or run. Design your own sponsorship form and provide information about how the money will be spent.

● Collect newspaper reports about wars around the world. What reasons are given for these conflicts?

● Write a letter to your local politician, asking him or her to support refugees. Some relief agencies, such as the UNHCR, rely on governments to donate money for their work.

● Contact a refugee family in your area. Invite them to come and talk to your class. Your friendship could make them feel more welcome in their new country and will help you understand the problems they face.

Finding out more

Visit the web sites of these organizations. Find out about their work and see how you can help.

The International Federation of Red Cross and Red Crescent Societies (IFRC)
Web site: www.ifrc.org
IFRC Secretariat
PO Box 372
CH-1211
Geneva 19
Switzerland
Telephone: 00 41 22 730 4222

The International Committee of the Red Cross (ICRC)
Web site: www.icrc.org
ICRC Public Information Division
19 avenue de la Paix
CH 1202
Geneva
Switzerland
Telephone: 00 41 22 734 6001

British Red Cross
Web site: www.redcross.org.uk
9 Grosvenor Crescent
London SW1X 7EJ
Telephone: 020 7235 5454

Oxfam
Web site: www.oxfam.org
Oxfam UK Head Office
274 Banbury Road
Oxford OX2 7DZ
Telephone: 01865 311311

Save the Children Fund (SCF)
Web site: www.oneworld.org/scf
Save the Children UK Head Office
17 Grove Lane
London SE5 8RD
Telephone: 020 7703 5400

Amnesty International (information on human rights)
Web site: www.amnesty.org
Amnesty International UK
99–119 Rosebery Avenue
London EC1R 4RE
Telephone: 020 7814 6200

The Refugee Council
(information on refugee issues)
Web site: www.refugeecouncil.org.uk
Refugee Council Head Office
3 Bondway
London SW8 1SJ
Tel: 020 7582 6922

United Nations High Commissioner for Refugees (UNHCR)
Web site: www.unhcr.ch
UNHCR Branch Office for the UK & Northern Ireland
Millbank Tower
21–24 Millbank
London SW1P 4QP
Telephone: 020 7630 1981

GLOSSARY

aid Resources given by one country, or organization, to another country. Aid is given to help people in an emergency and to make long-term improvements in their lives.

ally A country that is united with another through a treaty or agreement. Allied countries usually fight on the same side in a war.

blockade To block off an area so that no vehicles, ships or people can get through.

cease-fire An agreement between warring groups to stop fighting. This agreement is sometimes made while the different sides try to reach a peace settlement.

chemical weapon A weapon that releases gases or poisons into the air intended to harm or kill people.

civilian Someone who is not in the military.

Code of Conduct Guidelines for people to follow when there is a crisis.

drought A long period of time without rainfall.

election A vote to decide the government of a country.

ethnic An ethnic group is a group of people who share the same race, nationality, culture or religion.

Gulf War The war in 1990–91 between the United States and its allies and Iraq. The war began when Iraq invaded Kuwait.

hostage A person who is held prisoner by a warring side so that it can achieve certain demands, such as release of its prisoners.

human rights Rights that belong to everyone, such as the right to freedom of movement, shelter and education.

independent Free from rule by another country.

invade To send a force into another country with the intent to take over that country.

irrigation Supplying land with water using canals or ditches to improve crop growth.

land mine An explosive device that is placed in the ground and is usually set off when someone steps on it.

massacre The killing of large numbers of people.

Médecins Sans Frontières (MSF) A relief agency that offers medical help in a crisis. The name is French for 'doctors without borders'.

minority group A group that is racially different from the majority of people in a country.

persecution The poor treatment of people because of their race or religion.

pests Animals or insects, such as locusts, that damage crops.

prisoner of war A soldier who is captured and held prisoner by the enemy.

racism The belief that some races of people are better than others. People who believe this may treat other races badly.

Red Crescent A Muslim relief agency that is part of the Red Cross movement. Its symbol is a red crescent.

relief agency An organization that helps people when there

is a disaster and runs long-term projects to help people in poorer countries.

repatriation The sending back of people to their own country.

republic A country that has an elected person as its head, such as a president, rather than a king or queen.

revenge Harming someone because they have harmed you in the past.

sanction Action taken against a country because it has threatened world peace or ignored human rights. The idea is to punish the country to force it to change its policies.

Soviet Union A large country in Eastern Europe and Asia, made up of many different states. The Soviet Union split apart in 1991.

terrorist A terrorist is someone who uses violence to create fear and dread in the belief it will help in achieving an aim, such as overthrowing a government.

United Nations (UN) An organization of countries around the world that encourages world peace and offers help to people in a crisis.

Universal Declaration of Human Rights Part of international law that includes laws to protect the rights of refugees.

uprising The act of rebelling against a government or those in power.

warlords Military leaders who use force to take control of an area.

INDEX

First published in the UK in 1998 by
Belitha Press
An imprint of Chrysalis Books plc,
64 Brewery Road, London N7 9NT

This revised edition published in 2002

Copyright © Belitha Press Ltd 1998, 2002
Text copyright © Paul Bennett

All rights reserved. No part of this book may be reproduced or utilized in any form or by any means, electronic or mechanical, including photocopying, recording or by any information storage and retrieval system, except by a reviewer, who may quote brief passages in a review.

ISBN 1 84138 446 1 (hardback)
ISBN 1 84138 447 X (paperback)

British Library Cataloguing in Publication Data for this book is available from the British Library.

Printed in Hong Kong by South Seas

10 9 8 7 6 5 4 3 2   (hardback)
10 9 8 7 6 5 4 3 2 1 (paperback)

Photographs by: Cover: Associated Press. Inside: Reuters (STR, Erik de Castro, Gleb Garanich), Panos Pictures (Martin Adler, Neil Cooper, Peter Fryer, Jon Spaull), Sipa/Rex Features (James Baker), Denis Cameron/Rex Features, Juliet Coombe/Rex, DRC/M. Szabo, L. Gilbert/Sygma, Still Pictures (Ron Giling, Teit Hornbak, Gary Trotter), Mike Goldwater/Network, ICRC (Eric Bouvet, David Chancellor), Daily Mirror (P. Dutoit, Ligue, Till Mayer, F. von Sury), Fiona McDougall/Camera Press, MSF/Gamma/Noel Quida, Gamma/Frank Spooner (Antonello Nesca, Renaut Thomas), Helene Rogers/Trip, UNHCR (E. Brussard, A. Hollman, Y. Saita, L. Taylor, J. Zaprzala), UNICEF (Lemoyne, G. Pirozzi) (Case study material provided by British Red Cross, ICRC, MSF, UNHCR, Reuters)